Table Of Contents

Are you wondering if this course/book is tailored to your needs? If you fall into any of these categories:

1. You aspire to dive into multifamily or real estate investing, even with limited funds.
2. You're eyeing the residential side of multifamily investing, typically involving four units or fewer per property.
3. You're ready to roll up your sleeves, investing both physical and mental energy to see a project through. You're open to embracing innovative approaches that might deviate from the norm.

If you see yourself in these descriptions, you've found your spot! Rest assured, this is the right place for you.

Here are several compelling reasons to contemplate this avenue as you embark on your real estate investment journey:

1. **Tailored Design and Budget:** With this choice, you possess the reins to sculpt your project's design while choosing a location that seamlessly fits your budget.

It's like crafting your unique piece of the puzzle that aligns perfectly with your financial goals.

2. **Staggered Progress, Solid Strategy:** If traditional loans don't align with your current circumstances, fear not. Embrace the power of gradual progress. As funds trickle in, you can gradually develop different facets of your project. This tactical approach not only allows you to avoid shouldering a mortgage burden right from the start but also empowers you to take steady strides toward your vision.

3. **Craftsmanship and Skill:** For those wielding a toolkit of skills, this path holds allure. Should you possess the expertise to tackle specific tasks, you can roll up your sleeves and dive into the labor of love yourself. By outsourcing only what's beyond your realm, you stand to cut costs significantly. Of course, always remember to familiarize yourself with the regulations governing your area before setting off.

But that's not all—another avenue beckons: FHA financing. It comes with a modest upfront investment and a reduced physical labor quotient. Imagine this: you inhabit one unit while the other three become your rental canvas. Here, an intriguing possibility unfurls—a realm where living rent-free might not be just a dream. Those three units, like silent partners, potentially cover the mortgage and maintenance expenses, even leaving a little extra jingle in your pocket each month.

In the intricate world of real estate, options abound, each thread holding potential for growth and opportunity. So, whether you're crafting step by step or embracing FHA's helping hand, the path is yours to explore.

A Journey of Resourceful Transformation

In the year 2010, my life stood at a crossroads, a pivotal juncture that would forever define my path. As a single mother of three, deeply rooted in the architectural and construction management field in the Bahamas, I stood on the precipice of a radical decision that would unleash a series of transformative events. Little did I know, this audacious step would not only reshape my circumstances but would also set in motion a cascade of opportunities that would shape my future in ways beyond imagination.

With unwavering determination, I embarked on a daring move to Poteau, Oklahoma—a place unfamiliar, devoid of acquaintances, and without predetermined living arrangements. This leap of faith was driven by an unyielding desire to liberate myself from the constraints of traditional employment. As I left behind the familiar and embraced the unknown, I was met with challenges, resilience, and a chance to redefine my existence.

The decision to uproot my life and venture into the unfamiliar was not without its hardships. However, the rewards were as unexpected as they were substantial. By embracing change and shedding the weight of conventional norms, I managed to slash my living expenses by an astonishing 78%. This financial liberation breathed new life into my journey, offering the precious gift of breathing room to explore, reflect, and reimagine the future.

In the midst of this profound transformation, an unexpected twist introduced itself. In the summer of 2012, my sister shared with me the concept of tax deed properties—a revelation that would spark an epiphany and forever alter the trajectory of my story. Fueled by curiosity, I immersed myself in rigorous research, setting the stage for a journey that would lead me to acquire my very first tax deed property—a single lot.

With my three children, ages 2, 7, and 9, standing by my side, we embarked on a remarkable journey: the construction of a house from the ground up. This undertaking was more than just a physical structure; it symbolized a monumental stride towards self-sufficiency. By bidding farewell to the burdensome weight of exorbitant housing costs, we ushered in an era of newfound freedom and potential. This was the inception of my profound connection to real estate investment—a bond that would only strengthen with time as I glimpsed the vast panorama of opportunities that lay before me.

The subsequent years were a whirlwind of tireless contemplation, meticulous research, and hands-on action. As I sought ways to expand my horizons, I pushed the boundaries of my resourcefulness to unlock new realms of potential. It was during these transformative moments that the seeds of multi-family real estate development were sown—an intentional evolution that emerged from the crucible of my personal journey.

And now, as you embark on your own journey through these pages, I extend to you an invitation into the world that was birthed from years of relentless pursuit. Within the chapters that follow, I am thrilled to introduce you to the story that emerged from the crucible of exploration—the story that encapsulates the very essence of resourceful thinking and innovative approaches to real estate. Welcome to the tale of possibilities, the narrative of transformation, and the realm of multi-family investing for the resourceful thinker.

Multifamily Investing: A Pathway to Wealth Creation

Multifamily Investing revolves around the strategic acquisition and management of properties comprising two or more Living Units within a single Parcel of Land. In the realm of real estate, multifamily structures offer unparalleled potential, enabling investors to cultivate a diversified portfolio that generates sustainable returns.

For the purpose of this transformative program, our focus rests exclusively on multifamily properties classified as residential, firmly distinguishing them from their commercial counterparts. Our journey embarks with the understanding that the scope remains confined to properties with a maximum of four units per parcel of land.

Embrace this enlightening narrative, as it unfolds the captivating tale of a visionary woman poised to guide you through the intricate realm of multifamily investing. Armed with resourceful thinking and insightful strategies, her journey becomes a roadmap, leading you toward the realm of financial prosperity and empowerment. Welcome to a voyage where multifamily investing is not just a transactional endeavor but a profound endeavor in reshaping your financial future.

Resourcefulness: Our guiding star.

Resourcefulness is the bedrock upon which our journey to multifamily investing success is built. It is the unwavering commitment to finding innovative solutions, the ability to navigate uncharted territories, and the creative prowess that propels us forward, even in the face of challenges.

In the realm of multifamily investing, resourcefulness becomes our guiding star. It's the art of taking what might seem like limitations and transforming them into opportunities. When we encounter roadblocks, resourcefulness empowers us to navigate around them, to see beyond the barriers, and to seize hold of the untapped potential that lies within each situation.

Think of resourcefulness as your secret weapon, your arsenal of tools that empowers you to overcome any obstacle. It's the compass that directs your steps when the path ahead is uncertain. With resourcefulness by your side, no challenge is insurmountable, no difficulty too daunting.

As we embark on this journey, I will provide you with the steps, the roadmap that outlines our path to multifamily investing greatness. But here's the magic: it's your resourceful nature that will breathe life into these steps. It's your creative thinking, your ability to adapt and evolve, that will transform these instructions into actions that drive real results.

When we talk about using resourcefulness as our secret sauce, we're tapping into a wellspring of ingenuity that knows no bounds. We're harnessing the power of our collective imagination, our innovative thinking, and our determination to carve a unique path toward our multifamily investing dreams.

Resourcefulness isn't just about making do; it's about making more. More opportunities, more connections, more value. It's about taking what's available and amplifying it, turning it into a catalyst for growth and success. It's the mindset that propels us to think beyond the ordinary, to challenge the status quo, and to reshape the world around us according to our vision.

So, as we embark on this transformative journey, remember that resourcefulness is your companion, your confidant, and your co-conspirator in creating a reality that surpasses your wildest dreams. Embrace it, nurture it, and let it guide you as we breathe life into our multifamily investing aspirations.

Together, with resourcefulness as our north star, there's no limit to what we can achieve.

Our aim is to guide you beyond conventional thinking, fostering resourcefulness to make your real estate investing dreams a vibrant reality.

Here's a glimpse of what this course entails:

1. **Calculating Success:** We'll delve into the art of determining the right scale for your venture. Discover how to calculate the size of the building that aligns with your budget and time constraints. This knowledge ensures a smoother journey, alleviating stress as you construct your vision.
2. **Location:** Finding the perfect location. Unearth the tactics to identify affordable lots in areas with robust rental markets. Striking the balance between cost and opportunity will set the stage for success.
3. **Team:** Building is never a solitary endeavor. Learn how to assemble a dynamic team of professionals who'll contribute to transforming your blueprint into

reality. From architects to contractors, we've got you covered.

4. **Build:** Break down the construction process step by step. Whether you're opting for a gradual build to align with funding sources or a comprehensive construction timeline, you'll gain insight into each phase.

5. **Tenant:** Discover strategies for filling your units with desirable tenants. Dive into the nuances of tenant selection, understanding the spectrum of potential occupants, and how they impact your investment.

6. **Cash-Out:** We'll unveil the intricacies of extracting invested capital from your project. As tenants' contributions cover your mortgage and more, you'll learn to access profits and secure your financial foundation.

7. **Emulate:** Utilize your newly acquired funds to seed your next project. We'll guide you through channeling your cash-out proceeds to catalyze future success stories.

8. **Real-Life Deconstruction:** Experience a breakdown of one of my personal projects, navigating through actual numbers and the intricate funding process. Walk alongside a real-world scenario.

Together, we're embarking on a journey beyond limits, stretching the boundaries of what's possible. Through each chapter, you'll unearth insights, strategies, and a supportive community to foster your growth. This system isn't just about real estate; it's about nurturing your potential and propelling your ambitions into new horizons. Get ready to elevate your thinking, embrace innovation, and build the future you envision.

I am truly excited to share with you the essence and purpose behind this exceptional book. Within its pages, I aim to unveil a world of possibilities, granting you a unique and profound sense of control over your investment journey.

Picture this: a canvas of opportunities where you, as the artist of your investment, hold the brush. This book is your guide to wielding that brush with skill and finesse, allowing you to craft an investment that is as unique as you are. No longer confined by rigid norms, you are about to embark on a journey that will empower you to shape every facet of your real estate endeavor.

Imagine selecting the perfect location that resonates with your vision and aspirations. Whether it's the vibrant heart of the city or the tranquil outskirts, the power to choose is in your hands. As you turn the pages of this book, you'll uncover the art of strategically positioning your investment to maximize its potential, a skill that will undoubtedly set you apart.

But it doesn't stop there. Visualize stepping into the shoes of an architect, masterfully designing the layout of your project. The possibilities are boundless - from optimizing space utilization to creating an environment that resonates with your intended audience. Your investment isn't just a structure; it's an embodiment of your creativity and foresight.

And let's not forget the pivotal role of budgeting. With the tools and insights at your disposal, you'll become a value engineering virtuoso, seamlessly sculpting your project to fit within your financial parameters. As you delve into this book, you'll find yourself equipped with the knowledge and expertise to make every dollar count, without compromising your vision.

Before we dive into the practical steps, I urge you to liberate your imagination. Embrace the exhilarating freedom of thinking outside the box. Allow your mind to wander through the realm of endless possibilities. Envision properties that stand as testaments to your ingenuity, investments that capture the spirit of innovation and sophistication.

Remember, this book isn't just a guide; it's a gateway to a world where your investment isn't limited by conventions, but rather defined by your unique aspirations. As we embark on this journey together, I encourage you to embrace the role of the visionary, the architect, and the strategist. Get ready to paint your investment masterpiece, one brushstroke of creativity at a time. The limitless horizon of real estate investment awaits, and the pages of this book will be your compass. Welcome to a realm where imagination meets action, and your dreams take shape in ways you've never imagined.

Contract With Yourself

By signing this contract, I commit to taking decisive action and diligently following the steps outlined in the course/book. I understand that implementing the strategies is crucial for achieving the desired results. I acknowledge that progress requires effort and consistency. I am excited to embark on this transformative journey and will document my commitment by sending a picture of this signed contract to support@mtspath.com. Together, we'll pave the way to success

Sign: _____

Date:_____

CALCULATION

In the foundational stage of our system lies a critical and pragmatic step: the art of calculation. While this may evoke memories of school days and equations, rest assured, this math holds the key to your investment success. Think of it as laying the groundwork for a sturdy foundation, one that will shield you from potential pitfalls and pave the way for a smooth journey ahead.

Initial research:

When it comes to finding affordable land for sale, Google becomes your trusty guide. A quick search unveils the states with the most budget-friendly options. As of the creation of this course/book, here's a snapshot of some states that popped up in the results:

Arkansas

Alabama

Arizona,

Colorado

Mississippi

Missouri

New Mexico

Please take note: While this list might not cover your specific state, your current available funds might not enable you to kick-start things in your hometown. It's all about adapting and learning. Begin where your resources allow, even if it means starting in a different state. The key is progress – from where you are to where you want to be.

Alright, let's shift our focus to Arkansas as the prime example for this illustration.

Use this tax deed site https://auction.cosl.org/auctions to look for vacant land for less than $4,000. Remember we are just looking to gather data at this point.

Tax Deed Defined: Let's take a journey into understanding the concept of a tax deed, specifically in the state of Arkansas. Imagine a tax deed as a legal document that the government issues as a result of unpaid property taxes. It's like a notice saying, "Hey, we need you to pay your taxes!" If the property owner continues to not pay up, the government steps in and holds a special kind of auction, called a tax deed auction. At this auction, the government sells off the property to the highest bidder. So, in a nutshell, a tax deed is a way the government ensures they get the money owed to them while giving someone else the chance to own the property. It's like a financial tug-of-war where the government says, "Pay up or pass it on!"

Note: There are other sites that can be used to purchase the land where no bidding is necessary, but for the purpose of this exercise we will go with the site listed above.

After doing this exercise I found a piece of land in Crittenden County 85 feet x 135 feet. It is the perfect size and it is under our $4,000 budget.

Note: Check https://www.ushousingdata.com/housing-authorities/crittenden-county-ar to confirm there is a waiting list for Section-8 housing (this shows 1-2 years wait). This will give you a good idea if housing is needed in the area where we are looking to start your investment journey.

We will next head over to the website to find average rents https://www.ushousingdata.com/fair-market-rents/crittenden-county-ar scroll to the area that shows the average rent for studio, 1-bedroom, 2-bedroom, etc.

The rent for a studio is approximately $800, 1-bedroom $900, 2-bedroom $1,000 and 3-bedroom $1,300. We will save this information as we will need it later.

Armed with the knowledge we've amassed through our initial research, we stand poised to move forward – to the crucial juncture of obtaining the funds required to bring our project to life. This phase holds immense significance and demands a pragmatic outlook. It's a juncture that beckons us to take practical strides, translating our aspirations into tangible accomplishments. Let's dive in, ready to explore the financial intricacies that will serve as the bedrock for propelling our project into the realm of reality.

Student A - Sourcing Your Funds

This is the point where resourceful thinking comes into play. It's time to put on your thinking cap and consider all the legal avenues available for sourcing funds. Maybe credit cards, personal loans, contributions from family members, tapping into your 401k, utilizing tax returns, or even drawing from your savings account. Delve into where you might find the financial resources and calculate the total amount that you could potentially gather.

Student B - Building Up $35 Daily

Here's a simple equation for you: $35 a day. If you don't already have an extra $35 a day to spare, this is where your resourcefulness truly shines. Think outside the box and brainstorm ways to generate that extra income – perhaps through ride-sharing services like Uber, picking up overtime hours, or exploring side gigs. The aim is to funnel this additional $35 a day into your real estate journey, igniting your progress step by step.

Student C - Let's Talk Partnerships

If your savings aren't adding up fast enough to bring your project to fruition, there's a practical solution: One avenue worth exploring is partnering up with three trustworthy individuals. By splitting costs four ways this will alleviate the load.

Using the earlier land example, saving just $250 a month for four months, collectively with your partners, can significantly ease your financial load by 75%. This pattern holds true for every project stage.

You have the flexibility to engage any number of trustworthy individuals. This approach entails collaborating on a few projects with your reliable cohort before venturing solo. If your financial resources are limited, starting with trusted partners could be your stepping stone.

Remember, legalities matter. Consult a legal expert to draft a contract for you and your partners, ensuring clarity and protection for all involved.

Let's tackle a practical question: What size of building fits within your budget?

Now that we've outlined the steps to determine the size of the unit or units you can construct, let's break down the process. It's time to align your aspirations with financial feasibility.

To begin, the first step involves discovering the baseline cost per square foot for residential construction in your chosen location. Let's take Arkansas as our example for this exercise. This fundamental detail serves as the cornerstone of your project's financial blueprint. Let's dive into the specifics as we embark on this practical journey.

If you follow the link provided below, you'll find a breakdown of construction costs in Arkansas. The range varies, with the lower end being approximately $88 per square foot and the higher end around $113 per square foot. If we calculate the average of these figures, it comes to about $100 per square foot. You can access the details here: https://todayshomeowner.com/general/cost/how-much-does-it-cost-to-build-a-house-in-arkansas/

So, considering the local scenario, we'll take an average cost of $100 per square foot for your rental property's construction. In the industry, it's customary to include a buffer of 20% on top of this figure for overhead and profits. However, in your case, since you'll be overseeing the project yourself, we'll subtract that 20% from the $100. After all, you wouldn't want to charge yourself for managing the project and securing profits. This approach keeps things practical and efficient. This brings us down to $80 per square foot, a figure that truly reflects your project's cost after streamlining expenses.

Let's dive into the financial side of things. For students in category "A," let's say you've scoured all your resources and managed to gather $60,000. Impressive work!

Now, shifting our focus to students "B" and "C." Imagine you and your partners can set aside $35 a day for a solid 48 months. Crunching the numbers, that adds up to a projected savings of approximately $60,000. What does this mean? Well, in a mere four months, students "B" and "C" can secure their plot of land and gradually start constructing their units step by step, utilizing the funds they've pooled together. It's a strategic approach that sets them on the path to realizing their vision.

Let's break down the numbers step by step. First, we'll subtract the $4,000 land cost from the total of $60,000, which leaves us with approximately $56,000 earmarked for construction.

Next, we'll take that $56,000 and divide it by the estimated cost per square foot, which is around $80, factoring out overhead and profit. This calculation leads us to an available area of about 700 square feet for your unit or units.

With this space allocation, we have several options for unit configurations:

- (2) Studio Units: You can comfortably accommodate two studios at $1,600 total gross revenue.
- (1) One-Bedroom and (1) Studio: Another choice is a one-bedroom unit alongside a studio, totaling around $1,700 gross.
- (1) Two-Bedroom Unit: If you prefer a larger unit, a two-bedroom setup could be managed at around $1,000.
- (1) Three-Bedroom Unit: Alternatively, a three-bedroom layout can be considered totaling around $1,300 gross.

These figures lay out your potential choices, reflecting the square footage and budget parameters we're working with. Your preferences and needs will be key in finalizing the best configuration for your project.

Let's put the information we've gathered about the rental rates in Crittenden County to good use. Imagine that all the students opt for the practical (2) studio option, utilizing their budget to the fullest with 700 square feet per unit. This configuration could potentially bring in around $1,600 monthly gross, with each unit fetching $800 in gross income. Now, to expand the scope, adding two more units to this property follows a similar pattern, barring the need for additional land. This straightforward approach can result in four rental units thriving on a single lot.

In our strategic journey toward optimizing the profitability of your multi-family residence venture, it's essential to keep a clear focus on your ultimate objective. The pivotal aim here is to strategically position yourself to unlock the potential of each lot by maximizing its revenue-generating capacity. How do we achieve this? The answer lies in the concept of "four doors."

Why "Four Doors"?

The concept of "four doors" revolves around configuring each lot to encompass four separate housing units. This configuration ensures that the property retains its classification as a residential space. This classification is crucial as it opens the doors to various advantages, from zoning regulations to financing options. By having four distinct units on a single lot, you not only maximize the property's revenue potential but also tap into the efficiency of scale, effectively diversifying your income streams.

Diverse Configuration Possibilities:

While the duplex configuration we previously explored is a valid approach, it's worth noting that the concept of "four doors" doesn't rigidly adhere to a specific layout. Flexibility is key, and there are various ways to achieve the four-unit arrangement. Some of these configurations include:

1. **One + One + One + One:** This configuration involves creating four individual units, each distinct in its design and layout. This approach caters to a diverse range of tenant preferences, allowing you to attract a wider tenant pool.
2. **One + Three:** In this layout, you have one larger unit paired with three smaller units. This can be a strategic move if you're targeting a mix of smaller and larger households in your target demographic.
3. **Two plus Two (Duplex Example Above):** As we previously explored, the duplex concept involves two separate housing units under one roof. By duplicating

this configuration twice on the same lot, you create four independent units.

Sequencing Your Construction:

A pivotal aspect that shapes your multi-family property's development is the sequencing of your construction efforts. Your budget serves as the guiding light, influencing the order in which each unit is constructed. This financial strategy can play a critical role in managing your cash flow and ensuring that your resources are optimally allocated throughout the construction process.

By strategically considering your budget, you can prioritize which units to build first, ensuring that the core of your revenue-generating potential is unlocked step by step. This approach allows you to start generating income sooner while managing expenses effectively.

In the realm of multi-family property development, the concept of "four doors" encapsulates a visionary approach to maximizing revenue potential while maintaining the property's residential classification. By diversifying your configurations and strategically sequencing your construction efforts based on your budget, you are setting the stage for a financially rewarding and sustainable venture. Remember, the key to success lies in adaptability, innovation, and a deep understanding of your investment landscape. As you embark on this journey, armed with the knowledge of the "four doors" concept, you are better equipped to shape your multi-family residence into a prosperous and strategically designed asset.

LOCATION

Finding the Ideal Location for Your Multi-Family Residence

When embarking on the journey of constructing a multi-family residence, one of the critical factors that warrant thorough consideration is the location. The choice of location can significantly influence the success and profitability of your venture. In this guide, we will delve into the essential aspects of selecting the right location for your multi-family residence, focusing on the elements that align with the presented program.

Exploring Economically Viable States

As you begin your location search, it's prudent to cast your gaze upon states that boast a relatively low cost of living. To identify such states, Google can be your invaluable companion. Conduct research to compile a list of states that align with this criterion, as a lower cost of living often corresponds to more favorable investment opportunities.

Strategic Utilization of Housing Authority Data

Another step in the process involves accessing the websites of public housing authorities in the states you've shortlisted. Specifically, you're looking for information regarding waiting lists for housing assistance programs like Section-8. If you discover a waiting list in a particular area, it could indicate a demand for rental units, making that location a potential hotspot for your multi-family residence project.

Identifying Affordable Lots

With potential hotspots in mind, it's time to turn your attention to sourcing affordable lots within those areas. Platforms like Zillow and Craigslist can be excellent resources for finding available lots. By exploring the listings on these platforms, you can gain insights into the current market prices for lots in your desired locations. This information will be instrumental in determining the feasibility of your project from a financial perspective.

Analyzing Rental Potential

As you progress in your quest for the perfect location, it's essential to gather data on rental rates in the chosen area.

Access the housing authority database to understand the prevailing rental rates for units in the vicinity. This step is pivotal in evaluating the potential return on investment your multi-family residence can offer. If the numbers align favorably, you're one step closer to realizing a profitable venture.

The Crucial Aspect of Lot Inspection

While affordability is a key consideration, it's crucial to remember that "cheap" doesn't necessarily equate to a good deal. Once you've identified a reasonably priced lot, it's time to roll up your sleeves and inspect it. Alternatively, you can enlist the expertise of a professional to assess the lot's condition. During the inspection, be on the lookout for large holes, craters, or any other factors that might escalate the cost of preparing the lot for construction. Ensuring that the lot doesn't devour your entire budget for preparatory work is paramount.

Aligning Your Property Strategy with Your Business Model

Your chosen location should not only suit your financial projections but also align with your chosen business model. If your aim is to cater to a particular demographic, such as Section 8 tenants or the middle class, the location should reflect the preferences and needs of your target group. You might even deliberate whether your strategy involves venturing into neighborhoods with diverse profiles, which could influence the perception and attractiveness of your multi-family residence to potential renters.

A Conclusive Note on Location Choice

The significance of a well-chosen location cannot be overstated when it comes to multi-family residence construction. From economic viability and housing demand to affordability and alignment with your business model, every facet plays a role in determining the success of your venture. As you navigate the intricate landscape of real estate, armed with the insights provided in this guide, you are better equipped to make informed decisions that will steer your multi-family residence project toward prosperity and long-term profitability. Remember, the location isn't just an address; it's the foundation on which your real estate aspirations will flourish.

TEAM

Assembling Your Dream Team for Property Development

As your multi-family residence project gathers momentum, the time has come to forge a team that will transform your vision into a tangible reality. In this critical phase of your journey, you're about to embark on an expedition to find individuals and professionals who will not only be instrumental in the construction process but also share your commitment to excellence and strategic foresight. With each role meticulously chosen, you're paving the way for a harmonious and successful collaboration that will bring your project to fruition.

Crafting the Blueprint: Finding the Right Architects and Designers

The first piece of the puzzle involves translating your vision into blueprints and site plans. In this digital age, online platforms like Upwork provide a treasure trove of talented architects and designers. Armed with your concept and budget, you can source individuals who specialize in crafting detailed plans tailored to your requirements. These plans aren't merely lines on paper; they are the foundational sketches that will guide the construction of your multi-family residence. It's crucial to communicate your intention of potential future expansion so that the layout remains flexible and scalable.

Partnering with a Competent General Contractor: The Backbone of Your Project

The general contractor you select will be the linchpin of your project's success. Platforms like Craigslist and Angie's List offer avenues to find experienced professionals, and your strategy here is both strategic and calculated. You seek a contractor who possesses the ideal balance of competence and availability. Someone who can devote their attention to your project without being overwhelmed by numerous commitments. This balance ensures not only top-notch workmanship but also a willingness to negotiate for the best pricing. Your project is unique, and your contractor should reflect that uniqueness.

Navigating the Subcontractor Network: Skillful Specialists

In the intricate tapestry of property development, subcontractors play a crucial role. From plumbing to electrical work, each piece of the puzzle requires a skilled specialist. Your strategy here is discerning: you opt for subcontractors who provide labor-only services. This ensures that you have direct control over the materials used, enabling you to source them at bulk pricing from local home improvement stores. With your floor plan as the blueprint, you task these specialists with generating comprehensive material lists, setting the stage for cost-efficient procurement.

Sealing the Deal: Contracts, Permits, and Negotiations

With your team selected, contracts signed, and visions aligned, you're ready to embark on the actual construction phase. At this juncture, ensure that all bonds and insurance are in place, providing both you and your team with a protective safety net. The contractor takes the reins, pulling the necessary permits and crafting a schedule for material delivery. If, at this point, budgetary concerns arise, your resourceful thinking comes into play. Engage in negotiations, explore creative solutions, and seek ways to bridge the financial gap without compromising the quality of your project.

Exercising Oversight and Flexibility

If you possess the skills and expertise to oversee specific aspects of the construction, you have the power to do so. Hiring a framer, an electrician, and coordinating with a plumber can provide you with a hands-on approach. You might even entrust the contractor with specific tasks, such as permit acquisition and site inspections, ensuring that each stage adheres to your meticulous standards.

As you meticulously curate your team, every step you take is a testament to your strategic foresight and commitment to excellence. Your selection of architects, contractors, and specialists forms the backbone of your multi-family residence venture. With your budget in mind, your vision as your guide, and your resourceful thinking as your compass, you're sculpting a collaborative effort that will materialize into a property that stands as a testament to your innovation and diligence. From blueprints to permits, from negotiations to hands-on oversight, your team will orchestrate a symphony of creation, turning your dreams into bricks and mortar.

BUILD

Embarking on the construction voyage of an x-plex—a venture that intertwines innovation and profit potential—requires a deep grasp of the intricate intricacies that define this process. While construction generally treads a path of predetermined stages, acknowledging the geographic subtleties that mold the final outcome becomes paramount. Each county boasts its own tapestry of building regulations, often painting diverse construction methodologies. The brushes of cost calculations also wield great influence, leaving marks on decisions concerning crawl spaces and beyond. Moreover, the choreography of construction, choreographed by factors like weather, material availability, and skillful labor, can unveil variations in its unfolding. It's worth underscoring that this glimpse is but a brushstroke on the vast canvas of construction, teeming with nuances. Prior to setting sail on such a journey, consulting local authorities and evaluating personal skill reservoirs stand as anchors, given that building is a symphony requiring both virtuosity and safety consciousness.

The Dance of Construction Steps: Guiding Your Progress

1. **Site Preparation: Setting the Stage**
   - The land is cleared of natural elements and debris.
   - Temporary structures for workers and equipment stand as prelude to the construction spectacle.

2. **Foundation Work: Laying the Groundwork**
   - Earth surrenders its space through excavation.
   - Footings and foundation walls find their roots in dug trenches.
   - The concrete ballet takes center stage with forms and rebar.
   - The pouring of the foundation is the grand finale.
   - Walls rise in unity—concrete masonry units (CMUs) or poured concrete—blocking nature's intrusion.
   - Waterproofing is the costume, shielding against moisture's encore.

3. **Subfloor and Framing: Constructing the Framework**
   - A subfloor unveils itself over the foundation.

- The structural masterpiece assembles—walls, roof, and floors.
- The exterior sheath safeguards against weather's crescendo.
- Internal partitioning dances into place, defining spaces.

4. **Roofing: Enveloping Protection**

- Rafters or trusses join the architectural ensemble.
- Roofing materials unfold, a textured tableau.
- Flashing and weatherproofing waltz around roof penetrations.

5. **Windows and Doors: Inviting Entry**

- Windows and doors unlock the entrance to the narrative.
- Sealing conducts airtight and waterproof symphonies.

6. **Utilities and Rough-Ins: The Hidden Orchestra**

- Plumbing takes its stance with water supply and drainage.
- Electricity's tendrils reach, sketching wiring and outlets.
- HVAC's ductwork breathes life beneath.

7. **Insulation and Drywall: Cozying the Interior**

- Insulation's embrace cradles walls, floors, and attics.
- Drywall weaves the backdrop for interior stories.

8. **Interior Finishes: An Artful Encore**

- Doors, trim, and molding adorn interiors.
- Walls are painted or dressed in textured attire.
- Flooring materials stage a tactile showcase.
- Kitchens and bathrooms showcase their fittings.

9. **Exterior Finishes: Dressing the Exterior**

- Siding and finishes clothe the façade.
- The exterior palette is painted and perfected.
- Nature's backdrop takes its place—landscaping and grading.

10. **Final Touches: Bringing Harmony**

- Light fixtures, switches, and outlets illuminate the space.
- Inspections cast a critical eye to ensure compliance.
- The punch-list sways to its final tune.
- The final walk-through curates perfection.
- Permits and certifications, a seal of accomplishment.

Inviting Tenants: The End Is In Sight

As we stand here, the groundwork is laid, the building stands tall, but hold on, the show isn't over until those tenants put pen to paper, sealing the deal. This is where the real magic happens, a living testament to the skill and dedication that brought your x-plex into existence. So, while the structure is in place, it's the people who bring it to life and make it a true success.

Here is an assortment of essential skilled trades required throughout the construction process. This compilation will serve as your guide to identify the precise expertise required at each project stage. As you embark on your online quest to secure skilled trades, this resource will be an invaluable aid in aligning your needs with the right professionals.

1. Site Preparation and Foundation:
    - Excavation Contractor
    - Concrete Contractor
    - Foundation Specialist

2. Framing and Structural Work:

- Framing Carpenter

- Roofing Contractor

- Structural Engineer

3. Exterior Work:
   - Siding Contractor
   - Exterior Painter

4. Windows and Doors:
   - Window Installer
   - Door Installer

5. Plumbing and Electrical Rough-In:
   - Plumber
   - Electrician

6. Insulation and Drywall:
   - Insulation Contractor
   - Drywall Installer

7. Interior Finishing:
   - Finish Carpenter
   - Flooring Contractor

- Painter

8. Kitchen and Bathroom Installation:
    - Cabinet Installer
    - Countertop Installer
    - Plumbing Fixture Installer

9. Electrical and Plumbing Finalization:
    - Electrician (Final Connections)
    - Plumber (Final Connections)

10. Final Touches and Landscaping:
    - Trim Carpenter
    - Landscaper

11. Inspections and Permits:
    - Building Inspector

12. Quality Control and Final Walk-Through:
    - Quality Control Specialist

By collaborating with skilled professionals at each stage, you ensure a seamless and successful residential building project.

TENANT

When it comes to establishing a solid foundation for your property investment journey, certain aspects deserve careful attention, and one of these pivotal components is crafting a comprehensive lease agreement. This document holds substantial weight, particularly in the context of a future cash-out process when financial institutions might call for it. By delving into the details of this phase, you're preparing yourself for a seamless transition when the time comes to reap the rewards of your investment.

The Significance of a Proper Lease Agreement:

As you navigate the labyrinthine world of property investment, envision the lease agreement as a cornerstone, a legal instrument that safeguards your interests and outlines the terms of your tenant-landlord relationship. A comprehensive lease agreement ensures that the tenant is well-informed about their responsibilities and obligations while solidifying your rights as a landlord. This seemingly unassuming document becomes paramount when it's time to cash out, as finance companies will undoubtedly request it as a part of their due diligence process. Having a well-crafted lease agreement in place demonstrates your professionalism and commitment to maintaining a transparent and equitable rental relationship.

Strategizing Tenant Selection:

Venturing into the realm of tenant selection invites a realm of choices that are pivotal to the long-term success of your property investment. As you embark on this path, you'll find yourself at a crossroads, presented with various routes, each with its unique implications:

1. **The Housing Choice Voucher Program:** This government initiative can offer stability and guaranteed payments, but it requires compliance with program regulations.
2. **VA Housing:** Catering to veterans can be a rewarding endeavor, aligning with a sense of duty to those who've served the nation.
3. **Disability Housing:** Creating a space that accommodates individuals with disabilities contributes to social responsibility while catering to a specific demographic.

4. **Airbnb:** Exploring the realm of short-term rentals offers the potential for higher profits, but demands consistent management and a dynamic approach.
5. **Private Party Housing:** Leasing to private individuals fosters personal connections and flexible arrangements.

Intriguingly, the canvas isn't limited to one route; you have the latitude to blend strategies. Merging private party housing with Section 8 or combining Section 8 with Airbnb introduces a layer of complexity that requires careful consideration. Your choice hinges on your investment goals, risk tolerance, and the niche you aim to serve.

Prioritizing Tenant Screening:

Regardless of the path you tread, one universal truth remains: tenant screening is paramount. A comprehensive system is essential to ensure that your property is entrusted to responsible and reliable individuals. Background checks and credit evaluations are fundamental tools to gauge a tenant's financial history and character. Developing a rigorous screening process bolsters the quality of your tenant pool, mitigates risks, and contributes to a harmonious landlord-tenant dynamic.

The intricacies of tenant selection and lease agreements underscores the multifaceted nature of property investment. Crafting a robust lease agreement is akin to fortifying your investment fortress, ensuring that the legal groundwork is laid for a successful cash-out process in the future. Navigating tenant selection options, be it government programs, private parties, or innovative platforms like Airbnb, demands a strategic mindset aligned with your investment goals. Yet, the common thread woven throughout is the importance of tenant screening, a crucial filter that safeguards your investment and nurtures a prosperous landlord-tenant relationship. As you forge ahead in your property investment journey, remember that thorough preparation and strategic decision-making are your trusted allies on the path to success.

CASH-OUT

As you traverse this pivotal stage, the first decision awaits: will you opt to cash out as an individual or funnel your gains through your corporation or LLC? Irrespective of your choice, a non-negotiable prerequisite is ensuring your credit stands steadfast. If it's less than pristine, use the construction phase as an opportunity to mend it. A stable credit score not only assures the best interest rates but also unlocks a larger share of cash. Google becomes your ally, offering a trail of cash-out and refinance companies. These entities focus on your lease agreement, not your personal income, thus unraveling a path to favorable outcomes.

The process pivots around an appraisal report, an instrumental compass. While some companies might foot the bill, others entail a fee ranging between $500 and $1,200. Once your details intertwine with the appraisals, the closing ritual typically unfolds within 30 days. Imagine a scenario where the appraisal echoes back $90,000, basking your project in a glow $30,000 above its initial investment—a triumphant result.

The inner workings of cash-outs bear nuances. Unfortunately, you won't be able to grasp the full embrace of the appraised value; instead, most companies extend up to 85%. In our illustrative case, this translates to a cash-out of around $76,000, before the subtraction of fees. Navigating this terrain demands foresight: ensure that your mortgage payments remain comfortably low, preserving $100 to $300 per door post-mortgage, insurance, and maintenance obligations. Initiate the journey at the $100 mark, but work towards the $300+.

The entire situation described earlier serves as an illustration; your real-world outcomes might hold their own distinctive story.

EMULATE

Take a pause. Let the journey wash over you. Reflect on the entire tapestry of this project, jotting down the elements you'd preserve and those you yearn to enhance. Once that list takes form, it's time to embark on a journey of emulation, carrying these insights as torchbearers to illuminate your path toward four doors at the chosen location.

Yet, remember, while this blueprint lays a foundation, there's a human pulse that defines this voyage. It's the ability to gaze beyond convention, thinking expansively, and unleashing resourcefulness that lends wings to your potential. As we unraveled the duplex tapestry in the earlier example, envision the threads of possibility weaving three studios instead. With a willingness to dig into research or seek mentorship, you unearth a route that makes multi-family investing feel like an open door.

Resourcefulness, the cornerstone of this endeavor, is an intrinsic trait within you. It's the secret ingredient that adds depth to this program's recipe for success. And if, by chance, you find solitary strides less comforting, consider the MTS

PATH one-on-one program—an outstretched hand, guiding you through every stride.

From discovering the perfect plot of land that aligns with your budget to designing layouts that embody your vision, our in-house team stands at the ready. We unravel the tapestry of:

- Project cost estimates
- Contractor sourcing tailored to your locality
- Fund-seeking guidance
- Lease Agreement
- Unveiling the key to having the bank back your venture

Eager to empower you for your next chapter, we're your stepping stones to crafting new beginnings.

Visit: www.lequipebuild.com

Call: 501-777-8537

BONUS

Don't have any savings? Don't worry, this approach is still within your reach. The numbers might appear different, but that's where my "Bite Size" method comes in. Imagine you have a desired end budget of $120,000. Now, if we subtract the land cost of $4,000, you're left with $116,000. Divide that by 80, and you're looking at around 1,430 square feet in total.

Here comes the fun part—you collaborate with a designer to bring your fourplex vision to life. The layout might encompass (1) 2-bedroom and (3) studio apartments. With this blueprint in hand, you tap into your contractor's expertise or rely on Google to break down your building budget into stages. Each stage factors in material and labor costs, creating a clear roadmap.

For instance, starting with the $5,000 land cost, you could allocate $10,000 for the foundation with plumbing rough-ins and $4,500 for wall framing, and so on, as you progress through the construction process. It's all about saving up for each stage and moving forward step by step.

Speaking of strategies, here's a gem for those inclined towards rehabilitating houses for investment. If you come across a house with two bedrooms and two baths, or even three bedrooms and two baths, consider this: divide that house into multiple units, craft several doors from that single building. Even if it has only one bathroom, weigh the cost of adding an extra one. This move could give you the opportunity to insert another door and boost your revenue streams.

So, whether you're starting from zero or exploring innovative ways to transform existing spaces, this journey is about adapting, planning, and making your real estate ambitions a reality.

I've got something really practical for you—a worksheet that's like your trusty sidekick. It's all about crunching those numbers to figure out how many units you need to make your units give you full-time support. It's like putting together a puzzle that's uniquely yours. This sheet is going to be your calculator, your strategist, and your cheerleader all rolled into one. Let's dive in and see how you can pave your way to that full-time dream with real numbers.

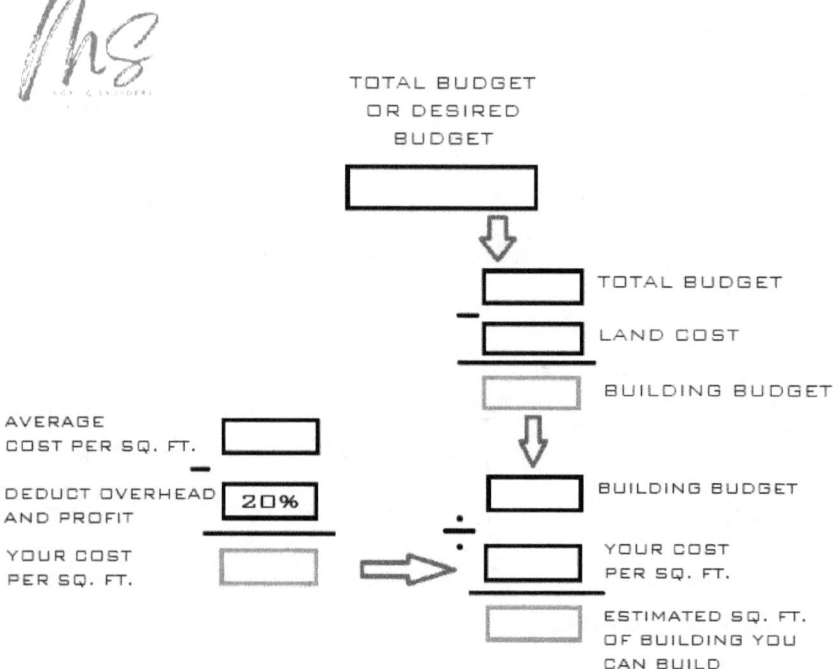

TOTAL BUDGET
OR DESIRED
BUDGET

TOTAL BUDGET

— LAND COST

BUILDING BUDGET

AVERAGE
COST PER SQ. FT.

— DEDUCT OVERHEAD
AND PROFIT   20%

YOUR COST
PER SQ. FT.

BUILDING BUDGET

÷ YOUR COST
PER SQ. FT.

ESTIMATED SQ. FT.
OF BUILDING YOU
CAN BUILD

USING THE ESTIMATED SQUARE FOOTAGE ABOVE, EXPLORE WAYS TO
LAYOUT YOUR BUILDING AND ARRANGE THE SQUARE FOOTAGE TO
YOU MAXIMIZE THE RENTS

PATH TO FINANCIAL FREEDOM

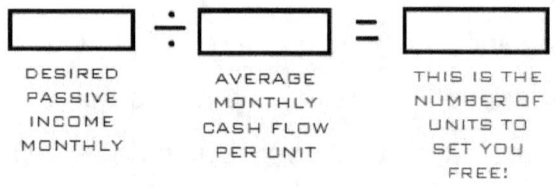

| DESIRED PASSIVE INCOME MONTHLY | ÷ | AVERAGE MONTHLY CASH FLOW PER UNIT | = | THIS IS THE NUMBER OF UNITS TO SET YOU FREE! |

Just like with any adventure you embark on, it's always a good move to reach out to the right authorities. They can help make sure you're sailing smoothly within the realms of Federal, State, and Local guidelines.

I'm truly grateful for the chance to chat about this idea with you. Wishing you heaps of luck on this exciting journey, and I'm eager to witness your projects come to life!

Thank You!

HELPFUL RESOURCES

Discounted lots for sale

1. www.zillow.com
2. www.landwatch.com
3. www.landandfarm.com
4. www.cosl.org
5. www.landmodo.com
6. www.landforsale.net
7. www.cheaplands.com
8. www.landflip.com
9. www.lotnetwork.com

Subcontractors or residential contractors for hire:

1. www.thumbtack.com
2. www.homeadvisor.com
3. www.angieslist.com
4. www.porch.com
5. www.houzz.com
6. www.buildzoom.com
7. www.craftjack.com
8. www.proreferral.com
9. www.networx.com

Building drawings and material lists

1. www.lequipebuild.com

2. www.upwork.com

3. www.freelancer.com

4. www.guru.com

5. www.architizer.com

6. www.thumbtack.com

7. www.houzz.com

8. www.toptal.com

9. www.99designs.com

10. www.peopleperhour.com

www.ingramcontent.com/pod-product-compliance
Lightning Source LLC
Chambersburg PA
CBHW062256290526
45794CB00006B/2576